Macramé

PLANT HANGERS, SHELVES, AND BASKETS

STACKPOLE BOOKS

An imprint of The Globe Pequot Publishing Group, Inc.
64 South Main Street
Essex, CT 06426
www.globepequot.com

Distributed by NATIONAL BOOK NETWORK
800-462-6420

© First published in French as *Macramé Suspensions Végétales* by Rustica, Paris, France—2023

PHOTOS :
COVER PHOTO : Claire Curt
CLAIRE CURT : pp. 12, 15–17, 20–21, 26, 29, 35, 45, 49, 51, 57, 63, 69, 77, 85, 95, 101, 109, 117, 122, 131, 138
VIRGINIE PUGLIESI : pp. 18–19, 22–24, 30–33, 36–42, 46–48, 52–55, 58–61, 64–67, 70–75, 78–82, 86–92, 96–99, 102–106, 110–115, 118–120, 124–128, 132–136.

DIRECTOR : Guillaume Pô
EDITORIAL DIRECTION : Élisabeth Pegeon
PUBLISHING : Chloé Herbin
ARTISTIC DIRECTION : Julie Mathieu
GRAPHIC DESIGN AND LAYOUT : Caroline Soulères
COPY PREPARATION AND CORRECTION : Nacima Bouzad
MANUFACTURING MANAGEMENT : Thierry Dubus
MANUFACTURE : Sonia Roméo
TRANSLATION : Nancy Gingrich/Mithril Translations

British Library Cataloguing in Publication Information available

Library of Congress Cataloging-in-Publication Data available

ISBN 978-0-8117-7474-1 (paper : alk. paper)
ISBN 978-0-8117-7488-8 (electronic)

∞™ The paper used in this publication meets the minimum requirements of American National Standard for Information Sciences—Permanence of Paper for Printed Library Materials, ANSI/NISO Z39.48-1992.

Virginie Pugliesi

Macramé

PLANT HANGERS, SHELVES, AND BASKETS

*Photographs by Virginie Pugliesi
and Claire Curt*

STACKPOLE BOOKS

Essex, Connecticut
Blue Ridge Summit, Pennsylvania

CONTENTS

PROJECTS

ABOUT THE AUTHOR

ACKNOWLEDGMENTS

INTRODUCTION

Macramé is an art based on a knotting technique. It is believed to have originated in the thirteenth century among Arab weavers and then developed everywhere else thanks to sailors who spread this technique they had learned to the rest of the world.

It really took off in the 1970s with the growth of handmade products, but like many other trends it gradually faded with the arrival of a new decorating style, giving macramé an old-fashioned, unattractive image.

In recent years, however, macramé has been making a comeback, driven in part by the arrival of Scandinavian decor, which goes well with soft, bohemian decorative elements. It is also gaining in popularity after a "green wave" emerged with the growing awareness of the importance of plants in our homes and their benefits to our physical and psychological well-being.

In this book, I invite you to discover the technique of macramé. A wide variety of plant hangers, some of which can also be used in outdoor spaces, will help you integrate a bit of nature into your home in a trendy, modern way.

Chapter 1

TOOLS, MATERIALS, AND BASIC KNOTS

TOOLS AND MATERIALS

To get started making macramé, you will need some very specific items.

CORD

First things first: cord! There are different types of macramé cord and different textures. Your choice should depend on your project and the final effect you're looking for.

I usually work with twisted cotton cord that, being both soft and supple, makes it easy to create knots, and it also has the advantage of fraying easily if you want to make fringe.

I also really like jute rope, which is stiffer and rougher than the twisted cotton but gives a rugged look and some character to your design.

From time to time, I also use combed cotton rope, which is very supple and, as its name suggests, is combed, making it easier to comb to make a straight, light fringe.

All of these are readily available from craft and hobby stores.

SUPPORTS

Once you've chosen your rope, you'll need a support on which to hang your project. You can use rings or wood gathered during walks in the forest or on the beach. You can also find various types in craft stores.

TOOLS

Once you've chosen your cord and the support, get a pair of good-quality scissors! It is important to have shears that are very sharp; they are well worth the higher cost.

Lastly, the item that is always close at hand when I'm creating is a tape measure. You use it to measure your cords or rope. You will want to calculate the amount needed before each project, according to the knots you plan to use.

One little extra thing is a macramé brush. It's very useful when you need to make fringe or tassels. But if you can't find one, a comb works just as well.

KNOTS

LARK'S HEAD KNOT

This is the basic knot for attaching your cords to a support.

Fold your cord in half and loop the folded end over and behind the support.

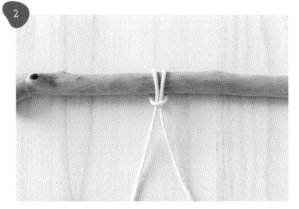

Insert both ends of the cord through the loop created and pull down to tighten the knot.

REVERSE LARK'S HEAD KNOT

Opposite of the regular lark's head, for this knot the loop is placed in front of the support.

SQUARE KNOT

One of the basic knots most often used in macramé.

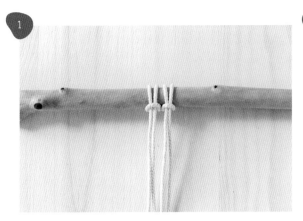

Take two cords. Attach each to the support using lark's head knots.

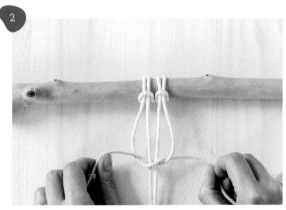

Place the left cord over the two center cords and the right cord underneath. Pass the end of the left cord through the right cord loop and the end of the right cord through the left cord loop. Tighten.

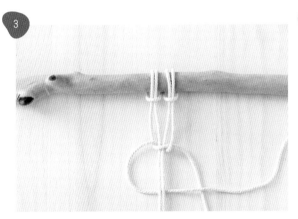

Then, conversely, place your left cord under the center cords and the right cord over the top.

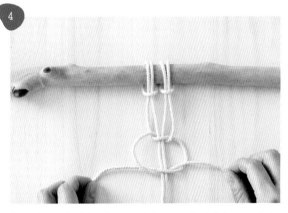

Pass the end of the right cord through the left loop and the end of the left cord through the right loop.

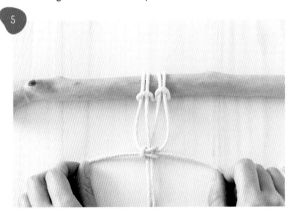

Tighten securely.

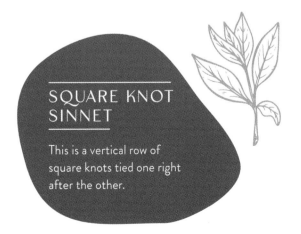

SQUARE KNOT SINNET

This is a vertical row of square knots tied one right after the other.

SWITCH KNOT

The switch knot is a variation of the square knot, made by simply switching the working cords and filler cords between each knot.

Take two cords. Attach each to the support using lark's head knots.

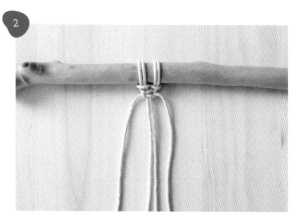

Make one square knot.

Move the outside (working) cords over and into the center of the two filler cords.

Tie the second square knot with the cords that are now on the outside.

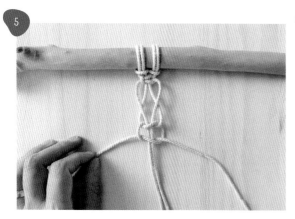

Make this second square knot, leaving a small space from the first one so that you can see the pattern forming.

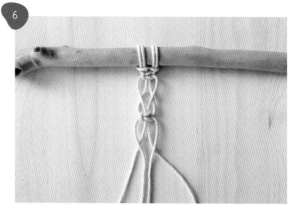

Continue in this way, changing the working cords for each new square knot.

ALTERNATING SQUARE KNOT

This technique connects two square knots together.

Attach four cords separately to the support using lark's head knots.

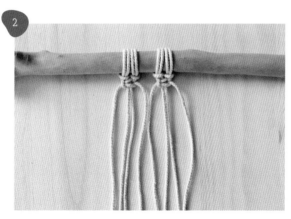

Tie two square knots side by side.

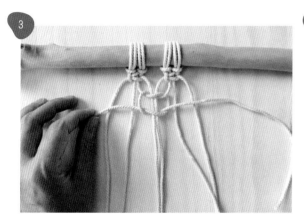

Use the last two cords of the first square knot and the first two cords of the second square knot to tie a new square knot between and below them.

Depending on the desired design, you can either tie the knot close to the other two or leave some space for a "net" effect.

HALF SQUARE KNOT (SPIRAL KNOT)

This is very often used to create a spiral.

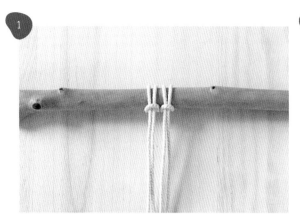

Attach two cords separately to the support using lark's head knots.

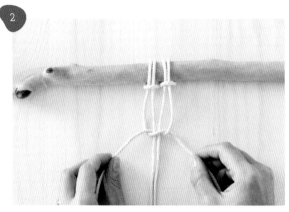

Place the left cord over the two center cords and the right cord underneath. Pass the end of the left cord through the right cord loop and the end of the right cord through the left cord loop.

Then, unlike the regular square knot, the position of the cords is not changed. Continue to pass the right cord under the center cords and the left cord over them.

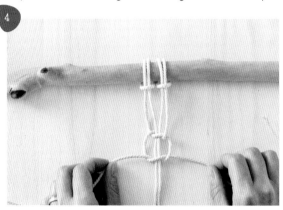

Pass the end of the left cord through the right loop and the end of the right cord through the left loop.

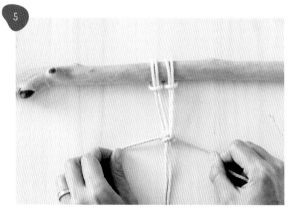

Tighten securely.

DOUBLE HALF HITCH KNOT (CLOVE HITCH KNOT)

This knot is very useful for creating patterns or adding dimension to your project.

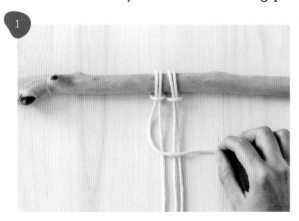

Attach two cords separately to the wood support using lark's head knots. Take the furthest left cord and place it over the other cords. This will be the filler cord.

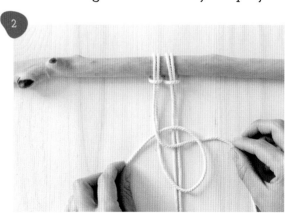

Take the second cord (working cord) and wrap it once up over and around the filler cord.

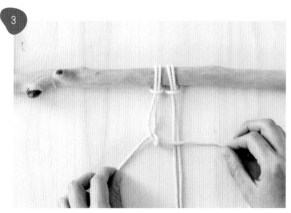

Tighten securely.

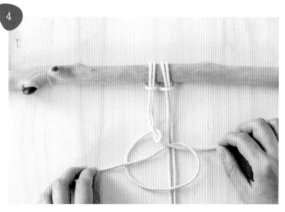

The half hitch knot must always be doubled. So, wrap the working cord around the filler cord a second time, being sure to bring the end of the cord through the loop formed under the filler cord.

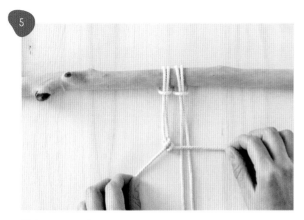

Tighten securely.

HORIZONTAL DOUBLE HALF HITCH KNOTS

To create this pattern, simply make a row of double half hitch knots horizontally.

Take the outside cord on the left or right side (depending on which direction you wish to create your row of knots). Place it horizontally and use it as your filler cord to make the double half hitch knots with the rest of the cords.

DIAGONAL DOUBLE HALF HITCH KNOTS

As with the horizontal knots, you will need to use the outside cord on the left or right side (depending on the direction you wish to work the knots). Place it diagonally toward the right or left, over the cords you wish to knot.

Use the cords to tie a series of consecutive double half hitch knots.

GATHERING KNOT

This is a very useful knot for tying a group of cords together and finishing a plant hanger.

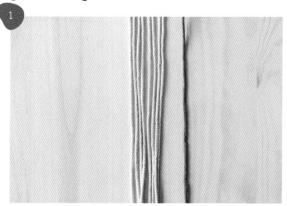

Cut a length of cord long enough to wrap around your group of cords several times (as many as you wish) to form the gathering knot. We'll call it C (the colored cord in the photos).

With one hand, grasp the group of cords as well as one end of C. C should stick out above your hand a bit.

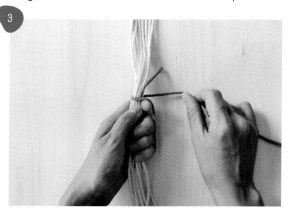

With your other hand, take the other end of C and bring it up to form a U-shaped loop, then start wrapping it down around the cords to be held together and around the loop.

Keep wrapping until a small loop remains through which you will pass the end of cord C. Tighten securely.

Take the end of C that you left sticking out at the top and pull up gently until the loop at the bottom is enclosed inside the wraps.

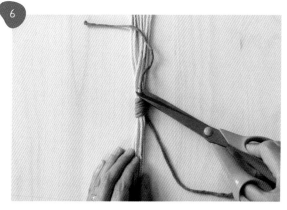

Trim off any excess of cord C at the top and bottom, if needed.

DIAMOND PATTERN

Four cords are needed to make this design.

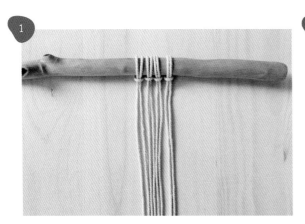

Attach the cords separately to your support using the lark's head knot.

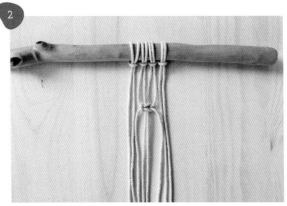

Make a square knot with the four center cords.

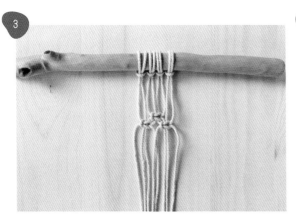

Under this knot make one alternating square knot to the left and one to the right.

Go back to the four center cords and make a square knot between the above two knots.

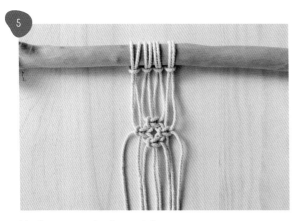

You have created a diamond shape.

Chapter 2

PROJECTS

BEADED
Plant Hanger

This pretty plant hanger is decorated with wooden beads for an original, soft bohemian style.

TOOLS AND MATERIALS

- 1 pair of scissors
- 16 wooden beads, ⅝ in. (15 mm) in diameter
- 7 wooden beads, ⅜ in. (10 mm) in diameter
- 3 pieces, 2.5 mm twisted cotton cord, 12 ft. (360 cm) long
- 1 piece, 2.5 mm twisted cotton, 14½ ft. (440 cm) long
- 1 piece, 2.5 mm twisted cotton cord, 3 ft. (90 cm) long (for the gathering knot)

Fold the three 12-ft. (360-cm) cords in half to find the center.

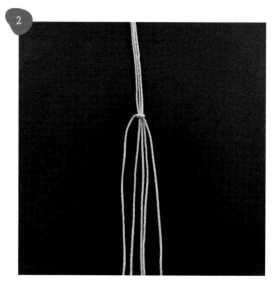

At about 2 in. (5 cm) from the center of the cord, take the 14½-ft. (440-cm) cord and use it to tie the three other cords together with an overhand knot.

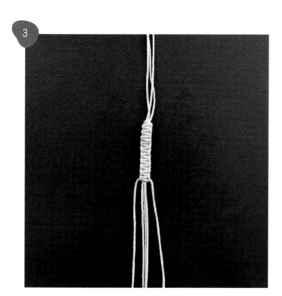

Using the strands from the 14½-ft. (440-cm) cord as working cords, tie a series of eleven consecutive square knots.

Bring the first and last square knots together to form a loop.

Use the longest two outside cords to make three consecutive square knots under the loop around the remaining six cords.

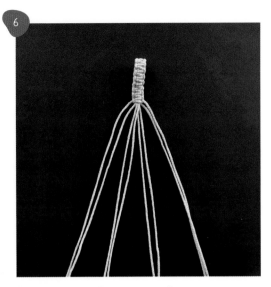

Separate your cords into groups of two.

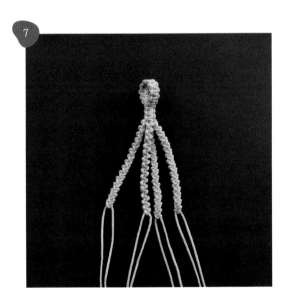

For each pair of cords, tie thirty alternating single half hitch knots. (In this case you will not double the half hitch knot.)

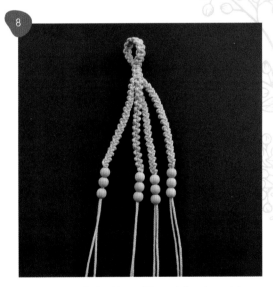

Take twelve of the ⅝-in. (15-mm) beads and insert three under each sinnet of single half hitch knots.

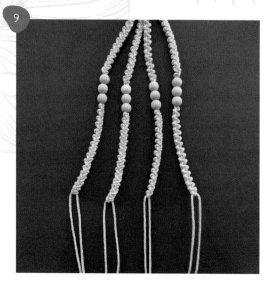

Tie another thirty alternating single half hitch knots under the beads added in the previous step.

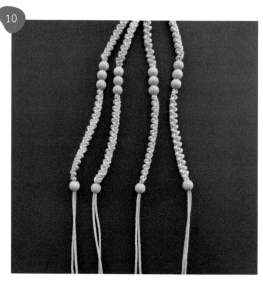

Take four of the ⅝-in. (15-mm) beads and thread one onto each pair of cords under this section of knots.

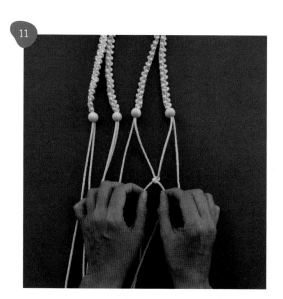

Between two beads, take the right cord under the left bead and the left cord under the right bead, and tie two alternating single half hitch knots about 3½ in. (9 cm) below the beads.

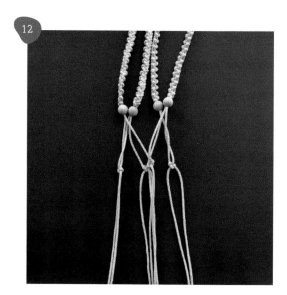

Repeat step 11 between all the beads (four knots).

Drop down about 3½ in. (9 cm) and use the 3-ft. (90-cm) cord to make a gathering knot.

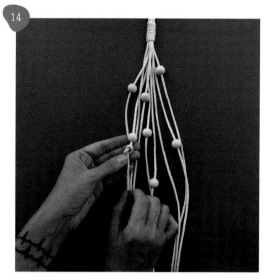

Take the seven ⅜-in. (10-mm) beads. Thread them on the cords under the gathering knot, at varying heights. Keep them in place by making an overhand knot under each one.

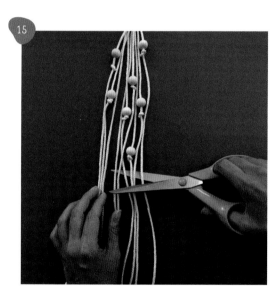

Cut the cords to make a tassel that is about 8 in. (20 cm) long.

TIP

You can absolutely use different sizes of beads.

WALL HANGING
with Shelf

Difficulty :
♦ ♦ ♦

Time required :
180 minutes

This pretty wall hanging has a shelf attached to hold small plants and decorative items.

TOOLS AND MATERIALS

- 1 pair of scissors
- 1 wooden dowel rod, ⅞ in. (21 mm) in diameter and 24 in. (60 cm) long
- 1 board for shelf, 6 x 20 in. (15 x 50 cm), with ¼-in. (6-mm) holes drilled in the corners
- 4 pieces, 2.5 mm twisted cotton cord, 5¼ ft. (160 cm) long
- 40 pieces, 2.5 mm twisted cotton cord, 4 ft. (120 cm) long
- 8 pieces, 2.5 mm twisted cotton cord, 15 ft. (450 cm) long
- 10 pieces, 2.5 mm twisted cotton cord, 10 ft. (300 cm) long
- 1 macramé brush

Take the four 5¼-ft. (160-cm) cords. Fold them in half and attach them to the wooden dowel using lark's head knots as follows: two cords in the center of the support and the other two on each end, 4¾ in. (12 cm) from the center cords. Tie a square knot under the two cords in the center.

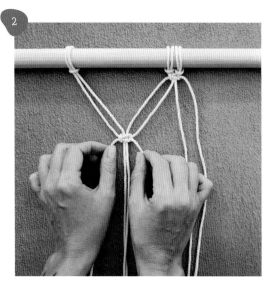

Take both strands of the cord on the left and the two left cords from the previous square knot. Tie a square knot 2¾ in. (7 cm) below the wooden dowel.

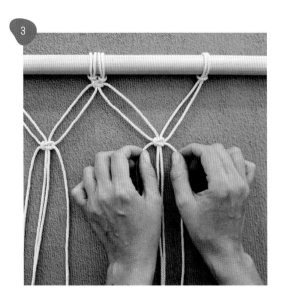

Take the two strands of cord on the right end and the two right cords from the square knot in the center. Tie a square knot 2¾ in. (7 cm) below the wooden dowel.

Take the right two cords from the square knot in step 2 and the left two cords from the one in step 3 and tie an alternating square knot 4¼ in. (11 cm) below the center square knot.

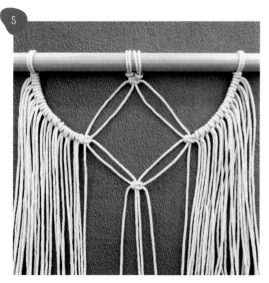

Take twenty-four of the cords that are 4 ft. (120 cm) long, fold them in half and attach twelve of them with a reverse lark's head knot to the two cords to the left of the square knot made from step 2. Attach the other twelve cords in the same way to the two cords to the right of the square knot from step 3.

Then take the remaining sixteen cords that are 4 ft. (120 cm) long. Fold them in half and attach them with a reverse lark's head knot to the two cords to the left and right of the square knot from step 4 (eight on the left and eight on the right).

Start this step off to the left side of your project. Take four of the 15-ft. (450-cm) cords and one 10-ft. (300-cm) cord. Fold them in half and attach them to the wooden dowel using lark's head knots, placing the 10-ft. (300-cm) cord in the middle of the 15-ft. (450-cm) cords.

Pick up the left strand of the 10-ft. (300-cm) cord. Use it as your filler cord and make a diagonal double half hitch sinnet to the left.

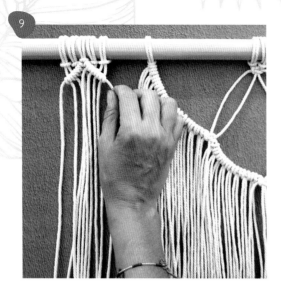

Pick up the right strand of the 10-ft. (300-cm) cord. Use it as your filler cord and work a diagonal double half hitch sinnet to the right.

Take the four cords at the center of the two diagonals and tie a square knot followed by an alternating square knot on the left and an alternating square knot on the right under the first square knot.

Tie a final alternating square knot in the center, under the two previous ones.

Pick up the left filler cord again and tie a diagonal double half hitch sinnet toward the right and use the right filler cord to make one toward the left, under the square knots. Connect the two diagonals with a double half hitch knot.

Make five more of these diamond patterns, repeating steps 8 to 12.

Starting under the last diamond, work one last diagonal double half hitch sinnet to the right.

Now move over to the right side of your project. Repeat steps 7 to 13. Then work a diagonal double half hitch sinnet toward the left under the last diamond.

Connect the two sinnets from steps 14 and 15 with a double half hitch knot.

Again, using the filler cords from the previous sinnets, work one double half hitch diagonal sinnet down toward the left and another down toward the right.

Tie a square knot with the strands from the last double half hitch knots worked on the left and right at the end of the diagonals, then use the same filler cords to work double half hitch diagonals from the right down toward the left and another from the left side down toward the right. Connect the two with a double half hitch knot to close the diamond.

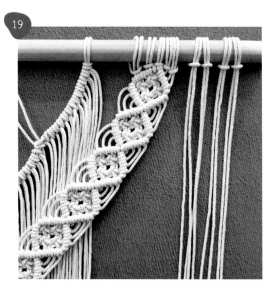

Take four of the 10-ft. (300-cm) cords. Fold them so that one side is 2 ft. (60 cm) long and the other is 8 ft. (240 cm) long. Attach them in pairs on the right side using lark's head knots, being sure to place the short strands in the center and the long strands to the outside of each pair.

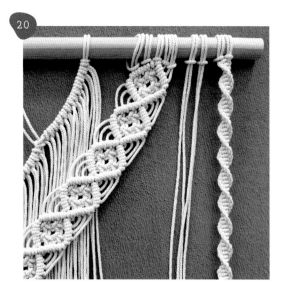

Using the pair of cords with short/long strands furthest to the right, tie left-facing half square knots to create a spiral that is 14¼ in. (36 cm) long.

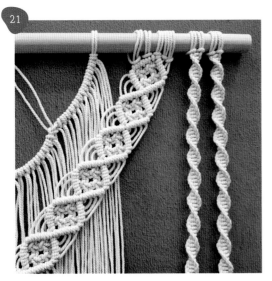

Take the second pair of cords with short/long strands. Tie left-facing half square knots to create a spiral that is 13½ in. (34 cm) long.

Take the last four 10-ft. (300-cm) cords and repeat steps 19 to 21 on the left side of your project.

Cut off the excess at the bottom of the center cords, giving it a V-shape. Set aside the scraps.

Use these snippets of cord to make a short fringe between the diamond shapes. Attach them using reverse lark's head knots. Trim the fringe to a length of about 1½ in. (4 cm).

Fray and brush the fringe.

Take the piece of wood that you'll be using as a shelf. Pass the center (filler) cords of the 14¼-in. (36-cm) spiral on the right through the hole at the corner of the shelf closest to you, leaving the others to go around the outside of the shelf. Tie five left-facing half square (spiral) knots to secure the spiral to the shelf.

Tie a small gathering knot under the mini spiral. Cut the cords to leave a 1½-in. (4-cm) tassel.

Repeat steps 26 and 27 on the back of the shelf with the 13½-in. (34-cm) spiral.

Repeat steps 26, 27, and 28 with the 13½- and 14¼-in. (34- and 36-cm) spirals on the left side.

TIP

You can use a piece of driftwood instead of a board for a more natural look.

CLASSIC OUTDOOR

Plant Hanger

Difficulty :
◆ ◇ ◇

Time required :
45 minutes

This basic plant hanger is a must-have in any home.

TOOLS AND MATERIALS

- 1 pair of scissors
- 1 wooden ring, 2¾ in. (7 cm) in diameter
- 6 pieces, ⅛ in. (3 mm) solid braided polypropylene rope (with core), 8 ft. (240 cm) long
- 2 pieces, ⅛ in. (3 mm) solid braided polypropylene rope (with core), 10 ft. (300 cm) long
- 1 piece, ⅛ in. (3 mm) solid braided polypropylene rope (with core), 28 in. (70 cm) long (for the gathering knot)
- 4 wooden beads, ¾ in. (20 mm) in diameter

Take the wooden ring. Attach the six 8-ft. (240-cm) ropes, folded in half, using lark's head knots.

Take the two 10-ft. (300-cm) ropes, folding each so one side is 4 ft. (120 cm) long and the other side is 6 ft. (180 cm) long. Attach one to the left of the cords from step 1 with a lark's head knot, placing the longer strand on the left outside edge, and the second on the right side with the longer strand on the right outside edge.

With the two outside strands (the ones that are longer than the others), tie one square knot around all the other strands. Tighten securely.

Then work five more consecutive square knots.

Separate your strands into groups of four. Tie a square knot with each group.

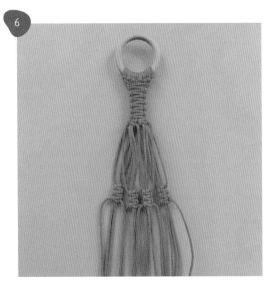

Drop down 4 in. (10 cm) and tie three square knots in a row with each group of four strands.

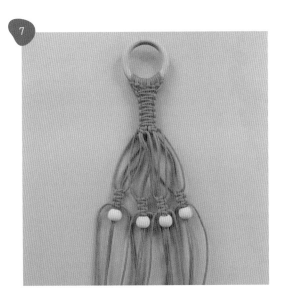

Take the wooden beads and insert the cords in the center of the square knots through the beads.

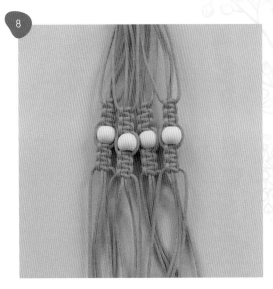

Work three more consecutive square knots under each bead.

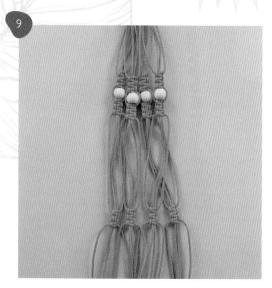

Drop down 5½ in. (14 cm) and tie three square knots in a row for each group of four strands.

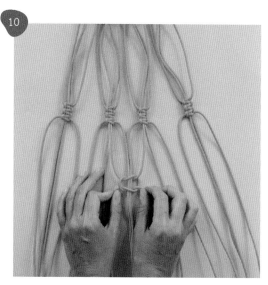

In between two of the sinnets of three square knots, use the third and fourth cords from the left sinnet and the first and second cords from the right sinnet and make an alternating center square knot 3 in. (8 cm) below.

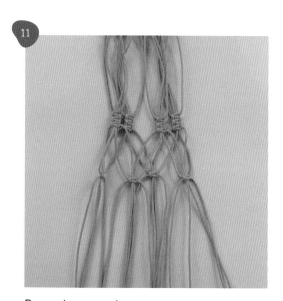

Repeat three more times.

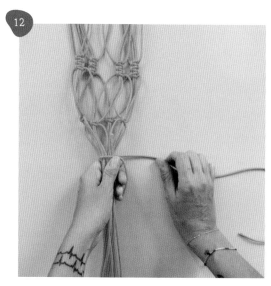

Take the 28-in. (70-cm) rope and make a gathering knot 3 in. (8 cm) below the last square knot.

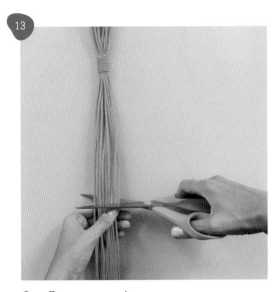

13

Cut off any excess cord.

TIP

Have some fun and change up the colors and the shapes of the wooden beads!

FRINGED
Plant Hanger

Difficulty :
◆ ◆ ◇

Time required :
120 minutes

This pretty plant hanger has lots of fringe to jazz up your decor!

TOOLS AND MATERIALS

- 1 pair of scissors
- 1 wooden ring, 2⅜ in. (6 cm) in diameter
- 8 pieces, 2.5 mm twisted cotton cord, 9 ft. (280 cm) long
- 2 pieces, 2.5 mm twisted cotton cord, 28 in. (70 cm) long (for gathering knots)
- 80 pieces, 2.5 mm twisted cotton cord, 8½ in. (22 cm) long (for the fringe)

Take the 9-ft. (280-cm) cords, fold them in half and place the wooden ring at their center.

Take one of the 28-in. (70-cm) cords and tie all the strands together with a gathering knot.

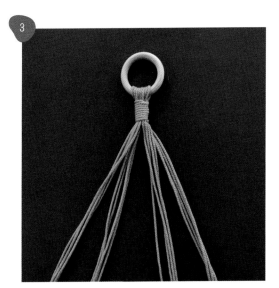

Under the gathering knot, separate the cords into four groups of four strands.

Tie a square knot with each group.

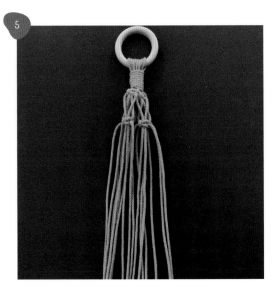

Drop down about 1 in. (3 cm) and tie a switch knot below the square knot from step 4. Do the same under each square knot.

Drop down another inch (3 cm) and tie a square knot under the switch knot. Do the same under each switch knot.

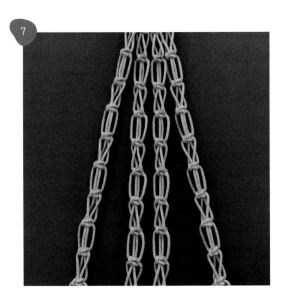

Continue alternating square knots and switch knots until you have made six switch knots and six square knots (you should end with a switch knot).

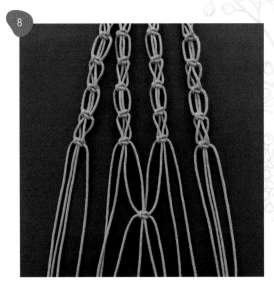

Drop down about 3.5 in. (9 cm). Working between two switch knots, take the last two strands from the left knot and the first two strands from the right knot and make an alternating square knot between the two knots.

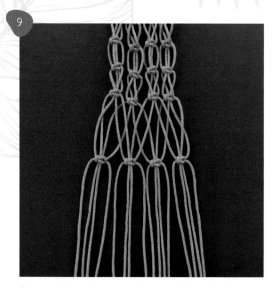

Repeat this step between the rest of the switch knots.

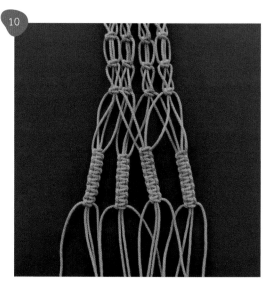

Under each knot from steps 8 and 9, tie seven more square knots, for a sinnet of eight square knots in all.

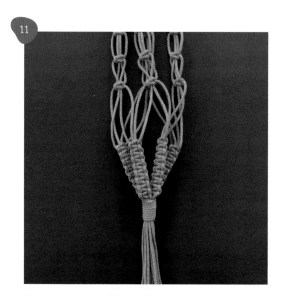

Take the second 28-in. (70-cm) cord and make a gathering knot, tying together all the cords under the square knot sinnets.

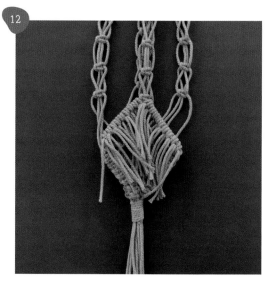

Take twenty of the 8½-in. (22-cm) cords, fold them in half, and attach them using reverse lark's head knots to the cords between the square knots from step 8 and the sinnet of square knots from step 10.

Repeat step 12 all the way around the plant hanger.

Fray the fringe and cut evenly along the bottom edge to form a cute, pointed shape.

Cut the cords under the gathering knot to make a pretty tassel.

TIP

You can play with the color of cord used for the fringe, to create a two-color plant hanger.

HANGING
Garden Shelves

This hanger, with several shelves perfect for pots of herbs, is ideal for your outdoor space.

TOOLS AND MATERIALS

- ◆ 1 pair of scissors

- ◆ 2 metal rings, 2 in. (5 cm) in diameter

- ◆ 3 boards for shelf, 6 in. (15 cm) wide and 12, 20, and 28 in. (30, 50, and 70 cm) long, with ¼-in. (6-mm) holes drilled in the corners

- ◆ 8 pieces, ⅛ in. (3 mm) solid braided polypropylene rope (with core), 20 ft. (600 cm) long

Fold four of the lengths of cord so that one side is 13 ft. (400 cm) long and the other is about 7 ft. (200 cm) long. Attach them to one of the rings with lark's head knots in the following manner: cords one and two with the longest side to the left and cords three and four with the longest side to the right.

Take cords two and three and tie fifty left-facing half square knots to create a spiral 8 in. (20.5) cm long.

Turn the ring over. With cords one and four, work a series of nineteen square knots to create a sinnet that is 6½ in. (17 cm) long.

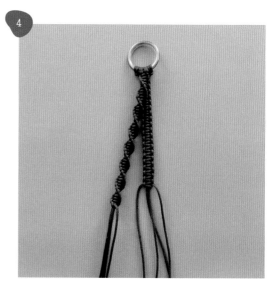

With the second ring and the remaining four cords, repeat steps 1 to 3.

Take the 12-in. (30-cm) board and the cords from one of the rings. Take the filler cords from the center of the spiral and pass them through the hole nearest you on the right.

Turn the shelf. Take the filler cords from the center of the square knot sinnet and pass them through the hole opposite the spiral.

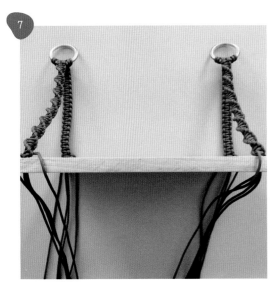

With the second ring, repeat steps 5 and 6 on the left side of the shelf.

Return to the spiral from step 5. With the outside cords work forty-four left-facing half square knots to make another spiral 7 in. (18 cm) long. Repeat this step with the cords in each corner.

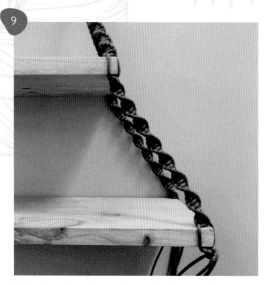

Take the 20-in. (50-cm) board. Pass the filler cords from the center of the spirals through the holes located on the right side of the shelf. Secure the cords by working two spiral knots.

Do the same on the left side of the shelf.

Again, tie forty-four left-facing half square knots to create two 7-in. (18-cm) spirals on the right.

Do the same on the left side.

Take the 28-in. (70-cm) shelf. Pass the filler cords from the center of the spirals through the holes located on the right side of the shelf. Secure the cords by working two left-facing spiral knots.

Tie a simple overhand knot under the mini spirals.

Cut off any excess cord, leaving about 2¾ in. (7 cm) for a tassel. Repeat steps 13 to 15 at each corner of the shelf.

TIP

You can use two different colors of rope, with one color in the front and the other in the back.

OUTDOOR LOG SLICE
Hanging Shelf

Difficulty :
◆ ◇ ◇

Time required :
60 minutes

A rustic log slice is transformed into a shelf to hold a pretty flowerpot.

TOOLS AND MATERIALS

- 1 pair of scissors

- 1 metal ring, 2⅜ in. (6 cm) in diameter

- 1 slice of wood from a log, 8½ in. (22 cm) in diameter

- 9 pieces, ⅛ in. (3 mm) solid braided polypropylene rope (with core), 9 ft. (280 cm) long

- 1 piece, ⅛ in. (3 mm) solid braided polypropylene rope (with core), 28 in. (70 cm) long

- 1 piece, ⅛ in. (3 mm) solid braided polypropylene rope (with core), 3 ft. (90 cm) long

Pass the nine 9-ft. (280-cm) cords through the ring and fold them in half so the center of the cords is on the ring.

With the 28-in. (70-cm) cord, tie a gathering knot under the ring around all the other cords.

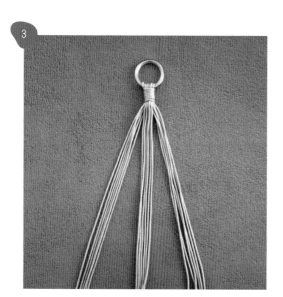

Separate the cords into three groups of six strands.

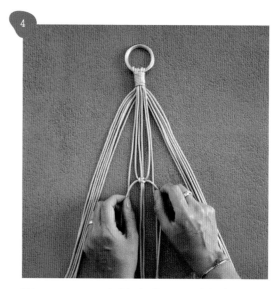

Take one group, and with the four strands in the center of the group, tie a square knot about 6 in. (15 cm) below the gathering knot.

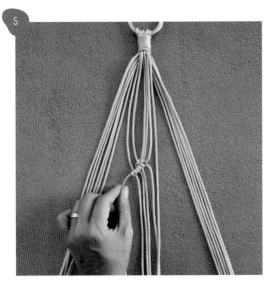

Find the cords in the center of the square knot. Using the left one as your filler cord, tie diagonal double half hitch knots down and to the left.

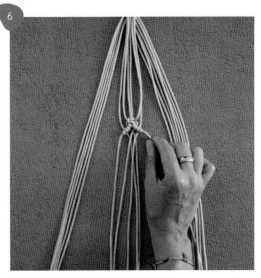

Then, taking the right strand to use as your filler cord, tie diagonal double half hitch knots down and to the right.

Take the two strands from the last double half hitch knots and tie a square knot.

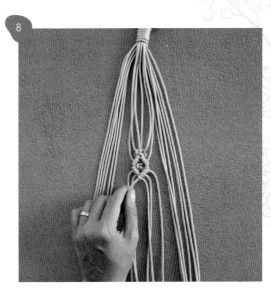

Go back to the filler cords and tie diagonal double half hitch knots going toward the left, then another sinnet going toward the right. Connect them with a double half hitch knot.

Under the diamond pattern, again use the four center cords to tie a square knot.

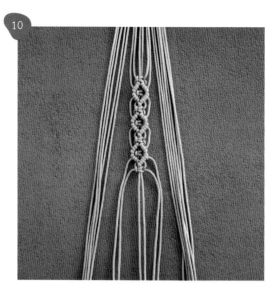

Repeat steps 5 to 9 two more times.

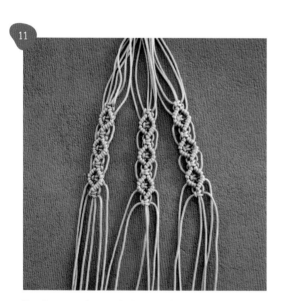

Do the same thing with the two other sets of six strands.

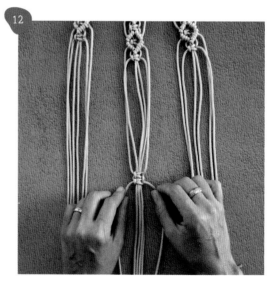

Go back to the first group of cords from step 4 (the center one). Drop down 6 in. (15 cm) and tie two consecutive square knots, using the two outside cords as working cords and the other four as filler cords.

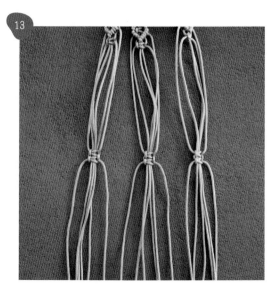

Repeat this step with the two other groups of cords.

With the 3-ft. (90-cm) cord, drop down about 4¾ in. (12 cm) below the last knots and tie a gathering knot.

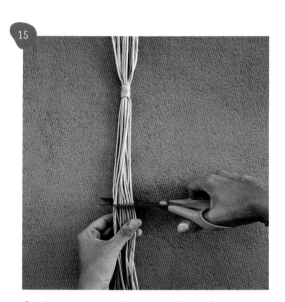

Cut, leaving a tassel of about 8 in. (20 cm).

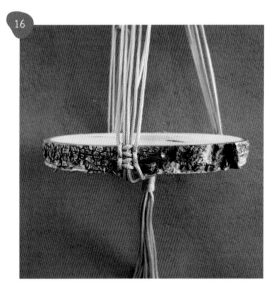

Take the log slice and place it in the holder. Your hanger is completed!

TIP

You can add wooden beads to the center of the diamonds in place of the square knots.

WALL
Basket

Difficulty :

◆ ◆ ◇

Time required :

180 minutes

A pretty basket to which we add a macramé pocket to hold dried flowers or very small green plants.

TOOLS AND MATERIALS

+ 1 pair of scissors

+ 1 round 12-in. (30-cm) wicker basket

+ 2 pieces, ⅛ in. (3 mm) twisted cotton cord, 20 in. (50 cm) long

+ 27 pieces, ⅛ in. (3 mm) twisted cotton cord, 63 in. (160 cm) long

+ 1 macramé brush (for final touches)

+ 1 jewelry pliers

Take the basket and one of the 20-in. (50-cm) cords. Attach the cord at opposite sides of the basket, going across the middle, with double half hitch knots.

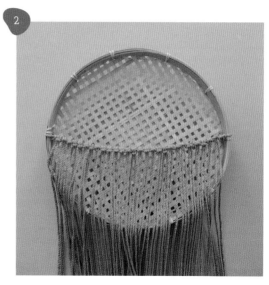

Take the 63-in. (160-cm) cords, fold them in half, and attach them to the cord from step 1 using lark's head knots.

Go to the first three cords. Pick up the third strand from the left and, using it as your filler cord, tie two diagonal double half hitch knots to the left, then two diagonal double half hitch knots to the right.

Pick up the fourth strand from the left and, using it as your filler cord, work two diagonal double half hitch knots to the right, then three diagonal double half hitch knots to the left.

Move to the next three cords. Repeat steps 3 and 4 to create a second diamond.

Then repeat these steps for the next twenty-one cords, to obtain a row of nine diamonds in all.

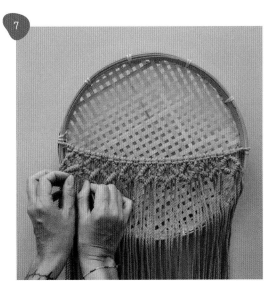

Go back to the first two diamonds. Tie a square knot with the four center strands located between those first two shapes.

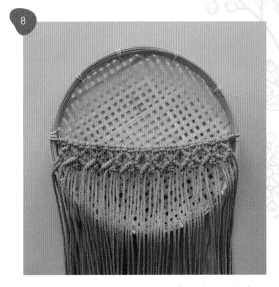

Do the same thing between each of the diamonds, for a total of eight square knots.

Go back to the center strands under the first diamond. Pick up the filler cords, and again repeat steps 3 and 4, to create a second diamond directly under the first one.

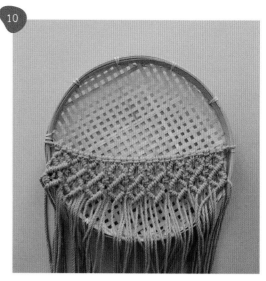

Do the same under all the other diamonds, to obtain a second row of nine diamonds.

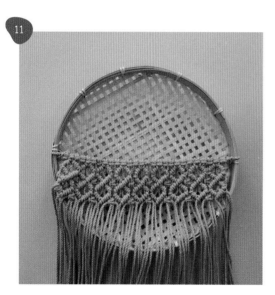

Tie a square knot between each of the diamonds.

Go back to the cords under the second column of diamonds. Pick up the filler cords and repeat steps 3 and 4 to create a third diamond. Do the same under the other diamonds, except for the last column, to obtain a new row of seven diamonds.

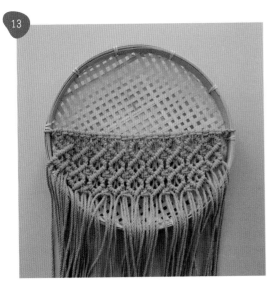

Tie a square knot between each of the diamonds.

Go to the cords under the third column of diamonds. Pick up the filler cords and repeat steps 3 and 4 to create a fourth diamond. Do the same thing under the other diamonds, except for the last column, to obtain a new row of five diamonds.

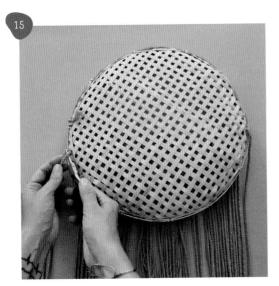

Turn the basket over and pull each cord through a small hole along the edge of the basket. Jewelry pliers can be used to grab the strands and pull them through.

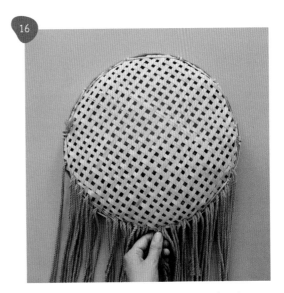

Pull on each strand to tighten the macramé pocket.

Take the remaining 20-in. (50-cm) cord. Use it as a filler cord and attach each strand to it under the basket using double half hitch knots.

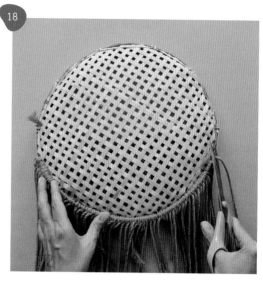

Tie an overhand knot at the end and cut off the excess cord.

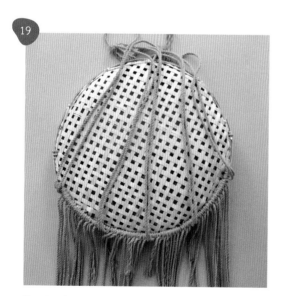

Starting from the left, set aside strands 1, 2, 15, 16, 27, 28, 39, 40, 53, and 54.

Take your scissors and cut the remaining cord to a length of about 2 in. (5 cm).

21

Fray each strand of cord.

22

Turn the basket back over and use the cord scraps to create mini tassels attached to the cords set aside in step 19.

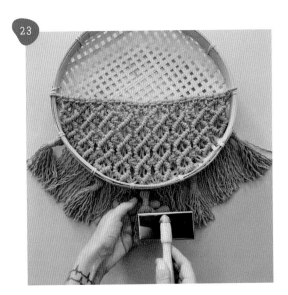

23

Fray and brush the tassels.

24

Trim the bottom edge to even everything out, and you are done!

TIP

You can skip the tassels and simply brush out the cords for a different finish.

BUTTERFLY
Plant Hanger

Difficulty :
◆ ◆ ◇

Time required :
60 minutes

A very pretty hanger with knots that look like butterflies, plus some bobbles to add style and dimension.

TOOLS AND MATERIALS

- 1 pair of scissors

- 1 wooden ring, 2¾ in. (7 cm) in diameter

- 7 pieces, 2.5 mm twisted cotton cord, 10 ft. (300 cm) long

- 1 piece, 2.5 mm twisted cotton cord, 13 ft. (400 cm) long

- 1 piece, 2.5 mm twisted cotton cord, 3 ft. (90 cm) long (for the gathering knot)

Pass the seven 10-ft. (300-cm) cords through the wooden ring and fold them in half over the ring.

Take the 13-ft. (400-cm) cord. Fold it in half to find the center and tie it around the seven other cords with an overhand knot.

Turn the project over so the knot is at the back. Use the strands of this cord to tie a left-facing half square knot (spiral knot) around all the 10-ft. (300-cm) cords.

Continue the left half square knots to create about a 2-in. (5-cm) spiral.

Separate the cords into groups of four strands. With one group of four strands make four square knots in a row.

Do the same with the three other groups of four strands.

Go back to the first group from step 5. Drop 4¾ in. (12 cm) below the last knot and tie a square knot.

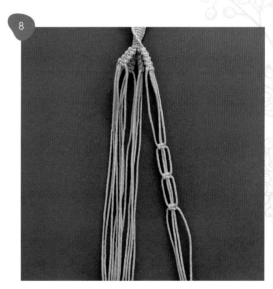

Drop down 1½ in. (4 cm) and make another square knot. Do this one more time.

With one hand, hold the strands in the center of the square knots, and with the other hand slide the square knots up until the three knots are all touching.

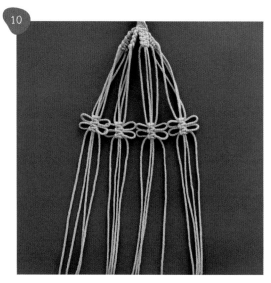

Repeat steps 7, 8, and 9 with the other groups of four strands.

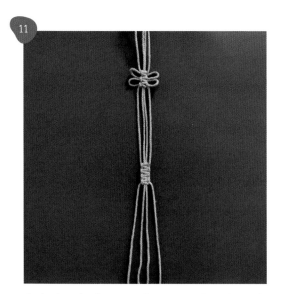

Go back to the first group from step 5. Drop down 4¾ in. (12 cm) again and tie four square knots in a row.

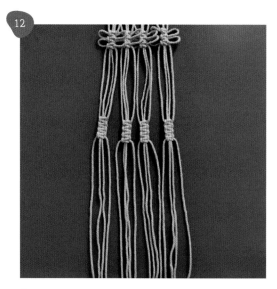

Do the same with the other three groups.

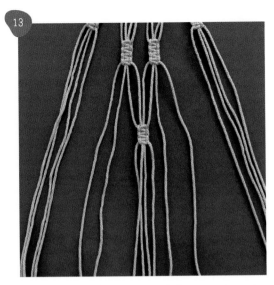

Move to a space between two of the square knot sinnets. Drop down 3½ in. (9 cm) and work an alternating square knot, followed by two more consecutive square knots.

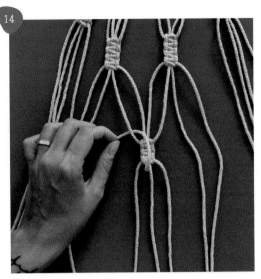

Take the left of the two cords in the center of the square knots. Pass it through the left loop above the first square knot.

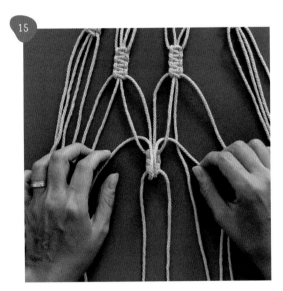

Take the right cord from the center of the square knots. Pass it through the right loop above the first square knot.

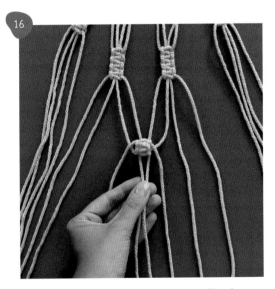

Bring the two cords back to the center. This forms a little bobble.

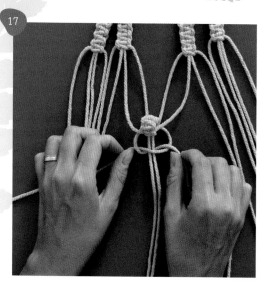

Take the outside strands and tie a square knot under the bobble. Tighten securely.

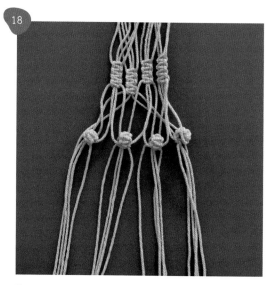

Repeat steps 13 to 17 three times.

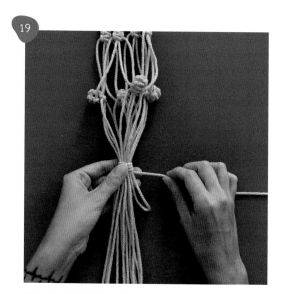

Take the 3-ft. (90-cm) cord. Drop down about 2¾ in. (7 cm) from the bobbles and tie a gathering knot.

Cut off the excess at the bottom of the cords, and you are done!

TIP

You can adjust the spacing of the square knots to make your butterfly "wings" larger or smaller.

WALL HANGING
Plant Holder

Difficulty :

◆ ◆ ◇

Time required :

60 minutes

This small wall hanging with a unique design is attached to a bamboo ring for a natural, modern look.

TOOLS AND MATERIALS

- ◆ 1 pair of scissors

- ◆ 1 bamboo ring, 8 in. (20 cm) in diameter

- ◆ 8 pieces, ⅛ in. (3 mm) twisted cotton cord, 10 ft. (300 cm) long

- ◆ 4 pieces, ⅛ in. (3 mm) twisted cotton cord, 6½ ft. (200 cm) long

- ◆ 1 piece, ⅛ in. (3 mm) twisted cotton cord, 2 ft. (60 cm) long

Take the eight 10-ft. (300-cm) cords. Fold them in half and, using lark's head knots, attach them to the top of the bamboo ring, preferably at the join to hide it.

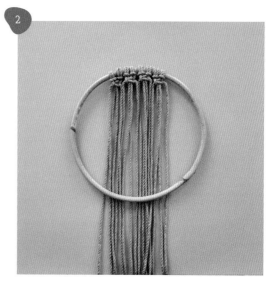

Taking two cords at a time, tie four square knots along the inside edge of the ring.

Tie three alternating square knots under the previous square knots.

Tie two alternating square knots under the square knots from step 3.

5

Tie one last alternating square knot under the square knots from step 4.

6

Starting on the left, attach your strands one by one to the bottom of the bamboo ring with double half hitch knots, using the ring as a filler cord.

7

Take the four 6½-ft. (200-cm) cords. Fold them in half and, using reverse lark's head knots, attach two to the bamboo ring to the left of the first double half hitch knot and two to the right of the last double half hitch knot.

8

Take the first strand on the left and, using it as a filler cord, tie horizontal double half hitch knots to the right with the next eleven strands.

Take the last strand on the right and using it as a filler cord, tie horizontal double half hitch knots to the left with the next eleven strands. Connect the two sides with a last double half hitch knot.

Under the first row of horizontal double half hitches on the left, set the first cord aside and take the second one to use as a filler cord. Tie horizontal double half hitch knots to the right with the next ten strands.

Under the first row of horizontal double half hitches on the right, set the last cord aside and take the preceding strand to use as a filler cord. Tie horizontal double half hitch knots to the left with the preceding ten strands. Connect the two sides with a last double half hitch knot.

Under the second row of horizontal double half hitches on the left, set the first cord aside and take the second one to use as a filler cord. Tie horizontal double half hitch knots to the right with the next nine strands.

Under the second row of horizontal double half hitches on the right, set the last cord aside and take the preceding strand to use as a filler cord. Tie horizontal double half hitch knots to the left with the preceding thirteen strands.

Take the filler cord from step 12 and tie diagonal double half hitch knots to the right with the next three strands. Then take the two strands from the last double half hitch knots and tie a square knot.

Go back to the filler cords and tie diagonal double half hitch knots to the left and the same to the right. Connect them to close the diamond.

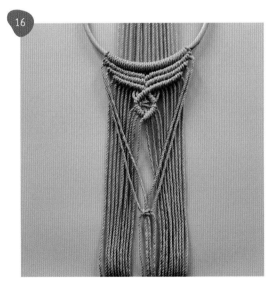

Take the first two and last two cords in the project. Tie a square knot 8 in. (20 cm) below the bamboo ring.

Take strands 3 and 4 and tie a left alternating square knot under the first square knot.

Take strands 21 and 22 and tie a right alternating square knot under the first square knot.

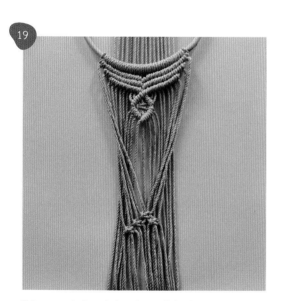

Take strands 5 and 6 and tie a left alternating square knot under the knot from step 17.

Take strands 19 and 20 and tie a right alternating square knot under the knot from step 18.

Under the two alternating square knots from steps 17 and 18, tie a center alternating square knot.

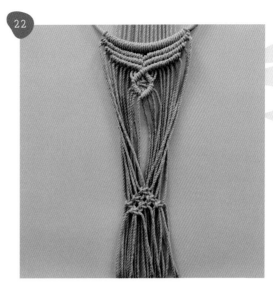

Under the two alternating square knots from steps 19 and 21, tie a center alternating square knot.

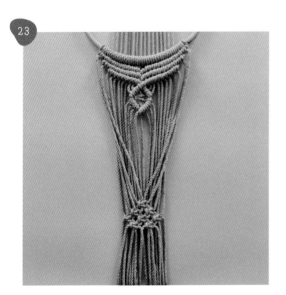

Under the two alternating square knots from steps 20 and 21, tie a center alternating square knot.

Under the two alternating square knots from steps 22 and 23, tie a center alternating square knot.

With the 2-ft. (60-cm) cord, tie a gathering knot 2¾ in. (7 cm) under the last alternating square knot.

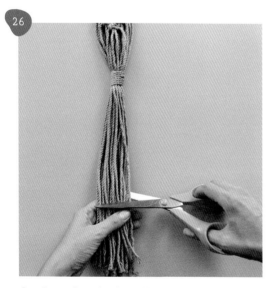

Cut the cords to the desired length, and you're done!

TIP

Feel free to experiment with different colors of cord.

OUTDOOR VINTAGE
Plant Hanger

Difficulty :

◆ ◆ ◇

Time required :

120 minutes

This plant hanger has a vintage design that is perfect for holding larger pots.

TOOLS AND MATERIALS

- 1 pair of scissors

- 1 metal ring, 2 in. (5 cm) in diameter

- 1 metal ring 2⅜ in. (6 cm) in diameter

- 8 pieces, 4 mm solid braided polypropylene rope (with core), 20 ft. (600 cm) long

- 8 pieces, 4 mm solid braided polypropylene rope (with core), 15 ft. (450 cm) long

- 1 piece, 4 mm solid braided polypropylene rope (with core), 28 in. (70 cm) long

- 1 piece, 4 mm solid braided polypropylene rope (with core), 3 ft. (90 cm) long

Take the smaller ring and pass the eight 20-ft. cords through it, folding them in half and placing the ring at the center of the cords.

Take the 28-in. cord and make a gathering knot just below the ring to tie all the cords together, then separate the strands into groups of four.

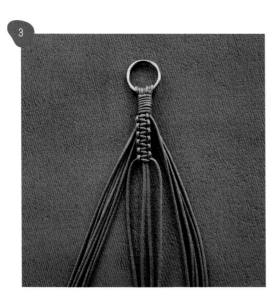

With one group of four strands, make a sinnet of six consecutive square knots.

Do the same thing with the three remaining groups of four cords.

5

Take the 2⅜-in. (6-cm) metal ring and position it below the last square knots.

6

Attach the ring to the cords, using the ring as the filler cord and working double half hitch knots.

7

Take the 15-ft. (450-cm) cords. Fold them in half and attach them to the ring using reverse lark's head knots. Place two between each square knot sinnet.

8

With the first group of four strands from step 3, below the double half hitch knots, tie a square knot with the four cords.

Take the two strands of the cord attached to the left of the square knot from step 8. Tie an alternating square knot to the left of the square knot just made.

Take the two strands of the cord attached to the right of the square knot from step 8. Tie an alternating square knot to the right of the square knot from step 8.

Tie an alternating square knot in the center of the two square knots just made.

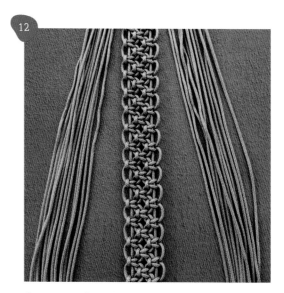

Continue working alternating square knots to the left, right, and center until you have completed twenty-seven left and right alternating square knots and twenty-six center ones.

Repeat steps 8 to 12 with the other groups of four strands.

Use the 3-ft. (90-cm) cord to tie a gathering knot around all the cords.

Cut off any excess cord at the bottom, keeping a 12-in. tassel, and you are done!

TIP

If you wish, use a different color for the 15-ft. (450-cm) cords, for a two-color hanger.

DOUBLE BASKET
Plant Hanger

Difficulty :
◆ ◆ ◆

Time required :
150 minutes

This large plant hanger has two bamboo baskets to hold two lovely plants. It definitely provides some boho vibes!

TOOLS AND MATERIALS

- 1 pair of scissors

- 2 bamboo rings, 6 in. (15 cm) in diameter

- 2 bamboo rings, 8 in. (20 cm) in diameter

- 1 wooden ring, 2⅜ in. (6 cm) in diameter

- 6 pieces, 2.5 mm twisted cotton cord, 13¾ ft. (420 cm) long

- 18 pieces, 2.5 mm twisted cotton cord, 4 ft. (120 cm) long

- 8 pieces, 2.5 mm twisted cotton cord, 2 ft. (60 cm) long

Pass the six 13¾-ft. (420-cm) cords through the wooden ring and fold them in half, placing the ring at their center. Take one of the 2-ft. (60-cm) cords and tie a gathering knot just below the ring to hold the group of six cords together.

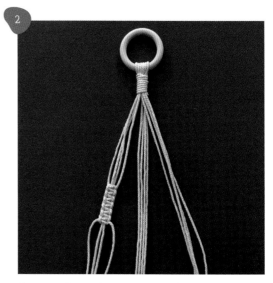

Separate the cords into groups of four strands. Take one of the groups, drop down 4¾ in. (12 cm) below the gathering knot, and tie a sinnet of six consecutive square knots.

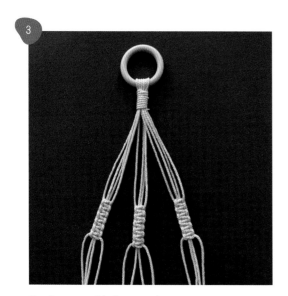

Do the same with the two other groups.

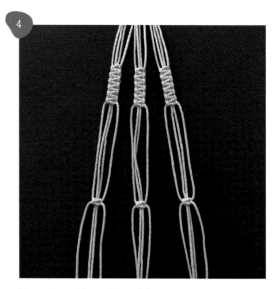

Drop down 4¾ in. (12 cm) below the last square knot and make another square knot. Do the same with each group.

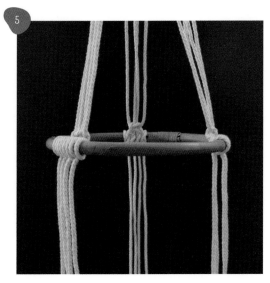

Take the first 6-in. (15-cm) bamboo ring. Place it under the square knots just made. Attach the strands to the ring with double half hitch knots, using the ring as a filler cord.

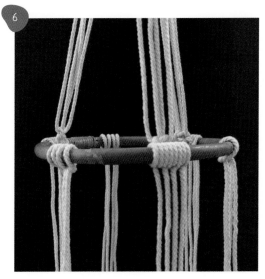

Take six 4-ft. (120-cm) cords. Fold them in half and attach them to the ring in pairs, between the double half hitch knots, using reverse lark's head knots.

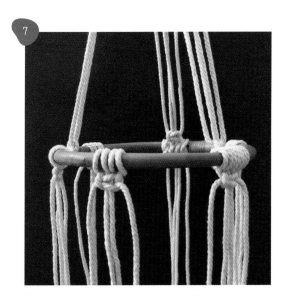

Tie a square knot under the double half hitch knots and under the lark's head knots on the pairs of cords that you just added.

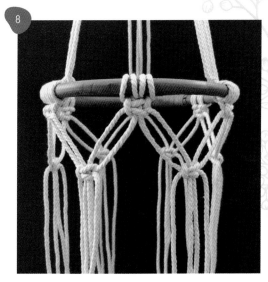

Between two of the square knots, take the last two strands from the knot on the left and the first two strands from the knot on the right, and make an alternating square knot between them, 1½ in. (4 cm) under the bamboo ring. Repeat this step all the way around the ring.

Between two alternating square knots, take the last two and first two strands of these knots and make a new alternating center square knot 2¾ in. (7 cm) below the bamboo ring. Repeat this step all the way around the ring.

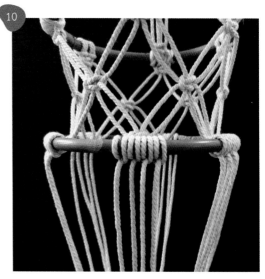

Take the second 6-in. (15-cm) bamboo ring and place it under the last square knots, attaching it to the strands with double half hitch knots, using the ring as a filler cord.

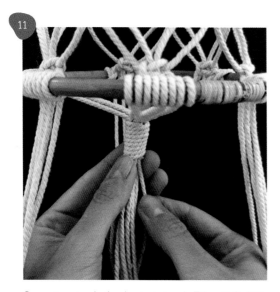

Separate out only the shortest strands. Take a 2-ft. (60-cm) cord and tie a gathering knot around these strands. Gently pull on each strand so they are stretched tight. Then cut to make a small 3-in. (7-cm) tassel.

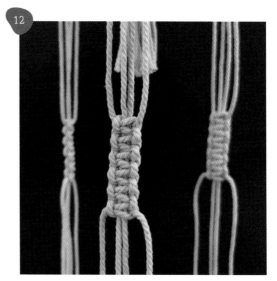

Go back to the long strands. With one group of four strands, tie a sinnet of six consecutive square knots, starting 4¾ in. (12 cm) below the bamboo ring. Repeat this step with each group of strands.

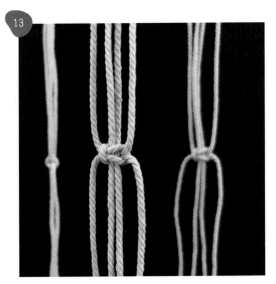

Dropping down another 4¾ in. (12 cm), tie another square knot under each square knot sinnet.

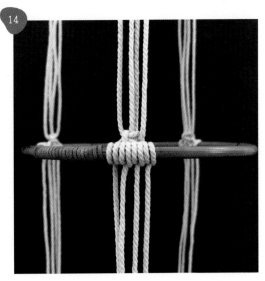

Take the first 8-in. (20-cm) bamboo ring. Attach it to the strands with double half hitch knots, using the ring as a filler cord.

Take the last twelve 4-ft. (120-cm) cords. Fold them in half and attach them to the ring using reverse lark's head knots. Group them in sets of four in the empty spaces on the ring, spacing the pairs 1½ in. (4 cm) apart.

Tie a square knot under the double half hitch knots and under the pairs of cords.

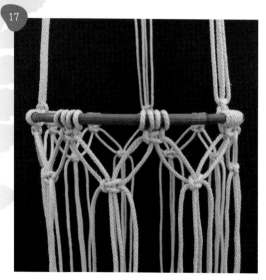

Between two square knots, take the last two and first two strands of those knots and make a new alternating center square knot 1½ in. (4 cm) below the bamboo ring. Repeat this step all the way around the ring.

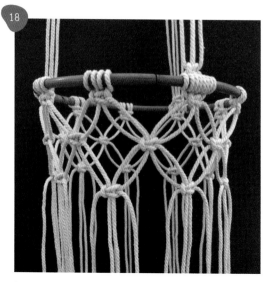

Between two alternating square knots, take the last two and first two strands of those knots and make a new alternating square knot 2¾ in. (7 cm) below the bamboo ring. Repeat this step all the way around the ring.

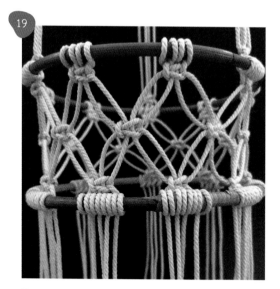

Take the second 8-in. (20-cm) bamboo ring and attach it to the strands with double half hitch knots, using the ring as a filler cord.

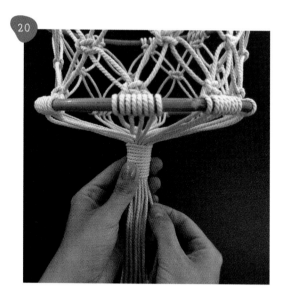

Take the last 2-ft. (60-cm) cord. Use it to tie a gathering knot, bringing all the cords together under the ring, pulling on each strand so they are stretched tight.

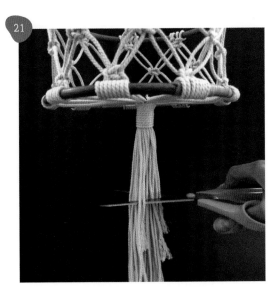

Cut your tassel to the desired length, and there you are, all finished!

TIP

You can make this plant hanger using metal rings rather than bamboo ones.

AIR
Plant Hanger

Difficulty :
◆ ◆ ◆

Time required :
150 minutes

The key word for this hanger is originality. This design is original because of its triangular shape and the plants it holds. Air plants are small plants that grow with no soil and just need to be sprayed with a little water every ten days.

TOOLS AND MATERIALS

+ 1 pair of scissors

+ 1 bamboo triangle, 11 in. (28 cm) wide

+ 3 wooden rings, 2⅜ in. (6 cm) in diameter

+ 16 pieces, 2.5 mm twisted cotton cord, 9 ft. (280 cm) long

+ 1 piece, 2.5 mm twisted cotton cord, 40 in. (100 cm) long

Take the bamboo triangle and four of the 9-ft. (280-cm) cords. Fold the cords in half and attach them to the top of the triangle with lark's head knots.

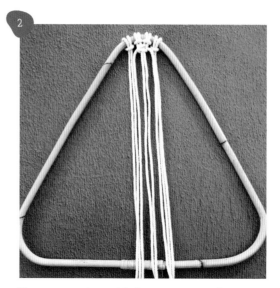

Tie one square knot with the two center cords.

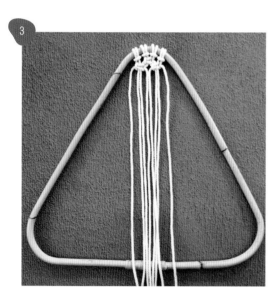

With the two left strands of this square knot and the two strands of the cord to the left, tie an alternating square knot on your left. With the two right strands of the first square knot and the two strands of the cord on the right side, tie an alternating square knot on the right.

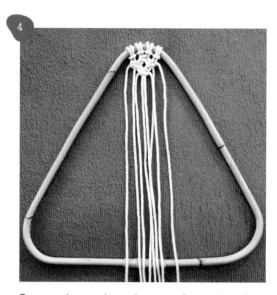

Between the two alternating square knots, tie an alternating square knot in the center.

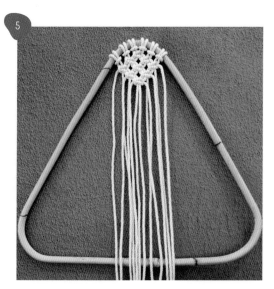

Take two more 9-ft. (280-cm) cords. Fold them in half and attach them to the triangle using lark's head knots, one on the left side and the other on the right. Starting on the left, make two alternating square knots going right. Then, moving to the right side, make three alternating square knots going left.

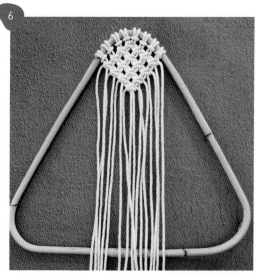

Take two more 9-ft. (280-cm) cords. Fold them in half and attach them to the triangle using lark's head knots, one on the left side and the other on the right. Starting on the left, make three alternating square knots going right. Then, moving to the right side, make four alternating square knots going left.

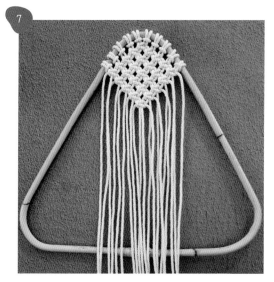

Take two more 9-ft. (280-cm) cords. Fold them in half and attach them to the triangle using lark's head knots, one on the left side and the other on the right. Starting on the left, make four alternating square knots going right. Then, moving to the right side, make five alternating square knots going left.

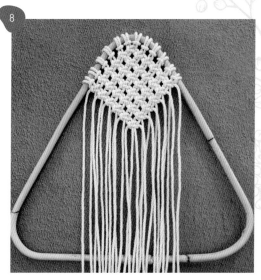

Take two more 9-ft. (280-cm) cords. Fold them in half and attach them to the triangle using lark's head knots, one on the left side and the other on the right. Starting on the left, make five alternating square knots going right. Then, moving to the right side, make six alternating square knots going left.

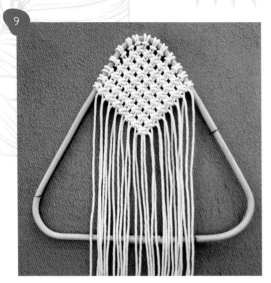

Take another two 9-ft. (280-cm) cords. Fold them in half and attach them to the triangle using lark's head knots, one on the left side and the other on the right. Starting on the left, make six alternating square knots going right. Then, moving to the right side, make seven alternating square knots going left.

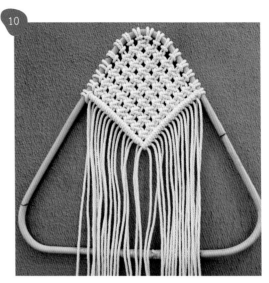

Take the last two 9-ft. (280-cm) cords. Fold them in half and attach them to the triangle using lark's head knots, one on the left side and the other on the right. Use the first strand of the left cord as a filler cord and work a diagonal sinnet of double half hitch knots going right. Repeat this step starting on the right, making a diagonal sinnet of double half hitch knots going left. Connect the two sinnets with a double half hitch knot.

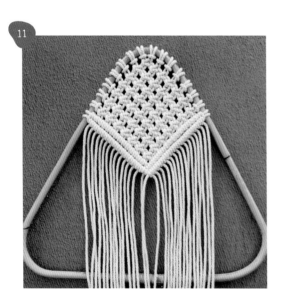

Go back to the left side. Take the second strand and work a second double half hitch diagonal below the first. Do the same on the right side. Connect the two diagonals with a double half hitch knot.

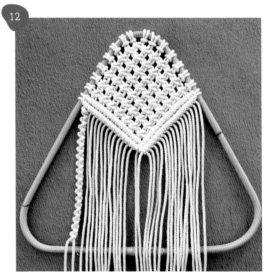

Go back to the left side. With the first two strands, tie a total of thirty-seven alternating single half hitch knots.

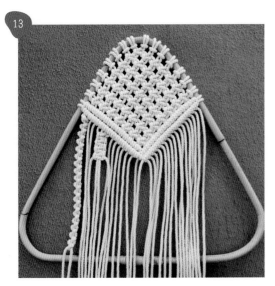

Skip two strands. Take the next four strands and make a sinnet of four consecutive square knots.

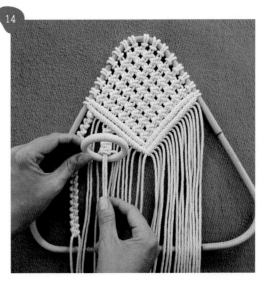

Take a wooden ring. Insert it below this sinnet, bringing the two center strands over the edge and into the center of the ring with the outside strands behind it.

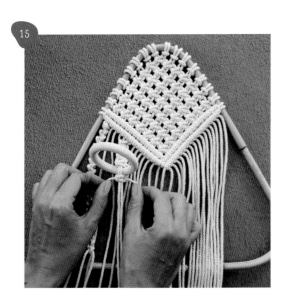

Tie a square knot just below the ring to secure it.

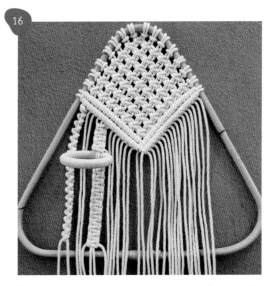

Make a sinnet of twelve consecutive square knots under the ring.

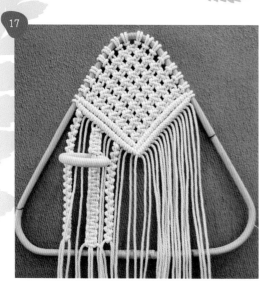

Skip two strands. Take the next two strands and tie a total of twenty-seven alternating single half hitch knots.

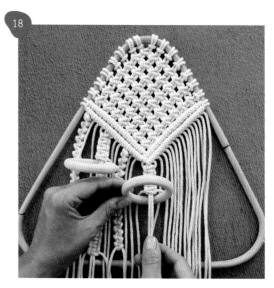

Skip two strands. Take the next four strands and make a sinnet of four consecutive square knots. Take a second wooden ring and insert it following the same instructions as in step 14.

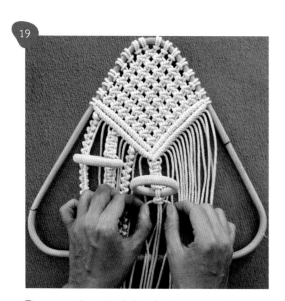

Tie a square knot just below the ring to secure it.

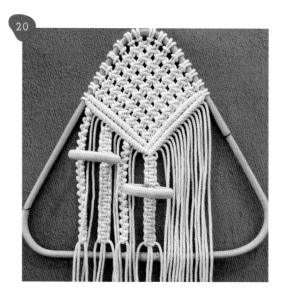

Make a sinnet of seven consecutive square knots under the ring.

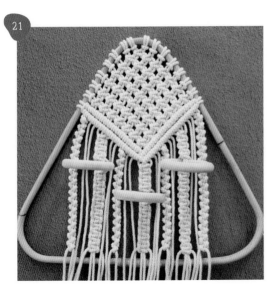

Move to the right side of the triangle and repeat steps 12 to 17, moving from right to left.

Going back to the left side, attach each of the strands to the base of the triangle with double half hitch knots, using the base as a filler cord.

Take the last cord, the 40-in. (100-cm) one, and tie a gathering knot to bring together all your cords under the base of the triangle. Pull on the cords a bit to tighten them and cut, leaving about 8 in. (20 cm) of cord for the tassel. And you are done!

TIP

Feel free to experiment with the colors of the cords and rings.

NO TASSEL
Plant Hanger

Difficulty :
◆ ◆ ◇

Time required :
60 minutes

This plant hanger is unique because it is made from the bottom up, so there is no tassel under your pot.

TOOLS AND MATERIALS

- 1 pair of scissors
- 1 wooden ring, 2⅜ in. (6 cm) in diameter
- 8 pieces, 2.5 mm twisted cotton cord, 13 ft. (400 cm) long
- 1 piece, 2.5 mm twisted cotton cord, 2 ft. (60 cm) long
- 4 large oval wooden beads, ¾ in. (20 mm) in diameter (with large holes)

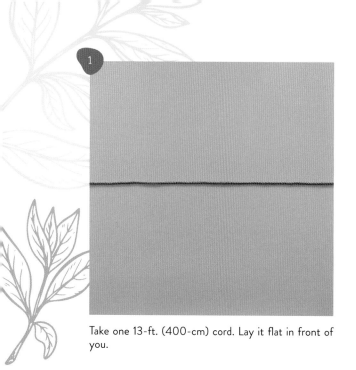

Take one 13-ft. (400-cm) cord. Lay it flat in front of you.

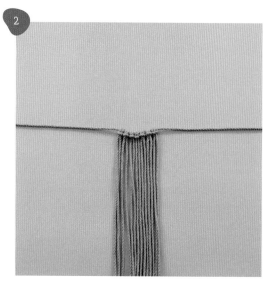

Take the seven other cords, fold them in half, and attach them to the center of the first cord using lark's head knots.

Take the two ends of the first cord and tie them together with a simple overhand knot, which will create a small circle.

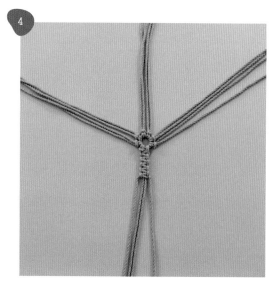

Separate the cords into groups of four strands. Take one group and tie five consecutive square knots.

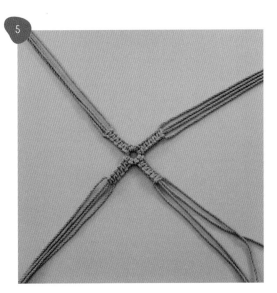

Do the same with the three other groups.

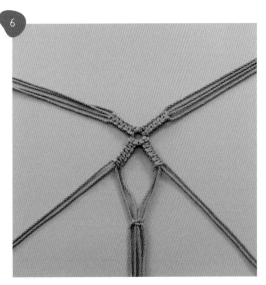

Position yourself between two of the square knot sinnets. Take the last two and the first two strands and tie an alternating square knot 3½ in. (9 cm) below the sinnets.

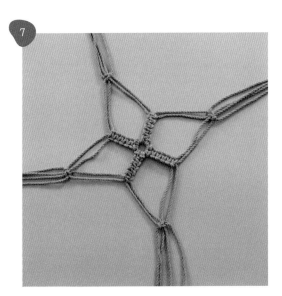

Do the same between all sinnets.

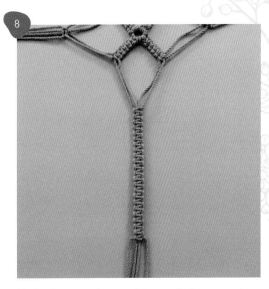

Under the square knot made in step 6, tie twenty-three consecutive square knots.

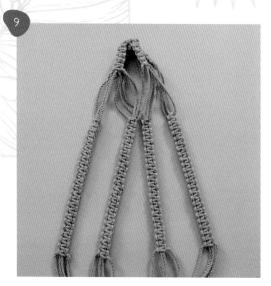

Repeat step 8 under the three other alternating square knots.

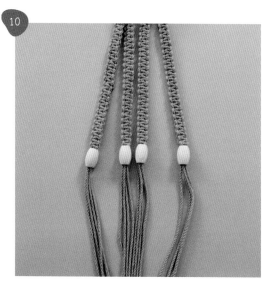

Take the ¾-in. (20-mm) oval beads and insert them under the last square knots made.

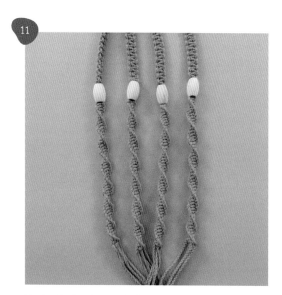

Under the beads, put the longest strands on the outside and the shortest ones in the center. Make a sinnet of right half square (spiral) knots to create a spiral that is as long as the sinnet of square knots above the bead. Do the same under each bead.

Take the wooden ring. Put all the cords through the ring and leave a little space between the end of your spirals and the ring for the gathering knot.

13

Take the 2-ft. (60-cm) cord and tie a gathering knot.

14

Cut off any excess length of cord. Your hanger is finished!

TIP

You may want to reverse the knots and start with the half square knot spirals instead. You may also decide to leave the excess cord at the top for a different style.

HANGING
Basket

Difficulty :
◆ ◆ ◆

Time required :
180 minutes

This hanging basket with a heavily knotted design conceals the pot inside.

TOOLS AND MATERIALS

- 1 pair of scissors
- 1 wooden ring, 2⅜ in. (6 cm) in diameter
- 2 metal rings, 6 in. (15 cm) in diameter
- 6 pieces, 2.5 mm twisted cotton cord, 11 ft. (340 cm) long
- 36 pieces, 2.5 mm twisted cotton cord, 5¼ ft. (160 cm) long
- 1 piece, 2.5 mm twisted cotton cord, 2 ft. (60 cm) long
- 1 piece, 2.5 mm twisted cotton cord, 5 ft. (150 cm) long

Take the six 11-ft. (340-cm) cords. Slide them through the ring and fold them in half over the side of the ring.

Take the 2-ft. (60-cm) cord and use it to tie a gathering knot just below the ring.

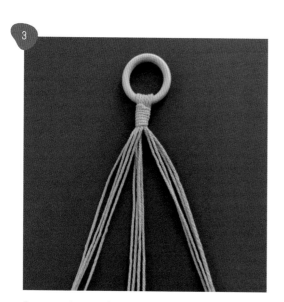

Separate the strands into three groups of four.

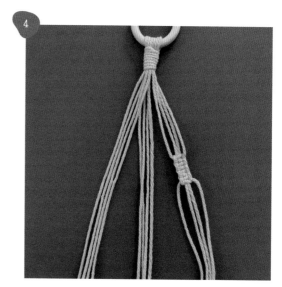

Take one group of four strands. Drop down 4 in. (10 cm) below the gathering knot and make a sinnet of four consecutive square knots.

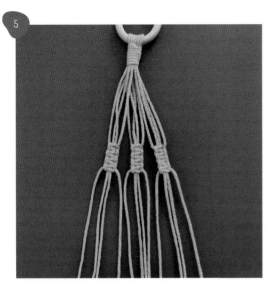

Do the same with the two other groups.

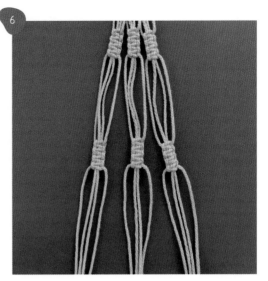

Drop down another 4 in. (10 cm), and again tie four consecutive square knots under the previous ones in all three groups.

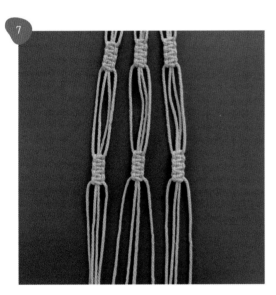

Drop down 4 in. (10 cm) once more and make a third series of four square knots under the second ones.

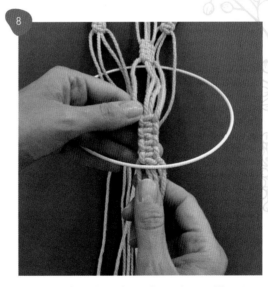

Take one of the 6-in. (15-cm) metal rings. Place it at the bottom edge of the last square knots.

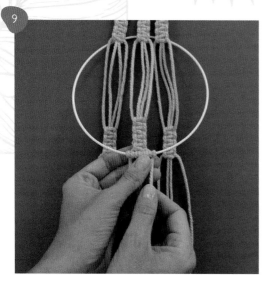

Use the ring as a filler cord and attach it to the cords using double half hitch knots.

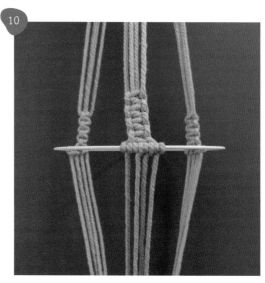

Leave about 5 in. (13 cm) between each group of cords.

Take twelve of the 5¼-ft. (160-cm) cords. Fold them in half and attach them to the ring using reverse lark's head knots in one of the 5-in. (13-cm) spaces.

Repeat step 11 in the other two spaces.

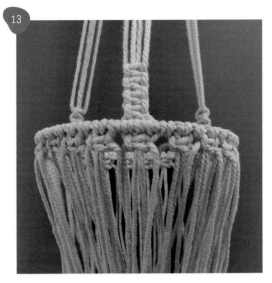

Take four strands at a time and tie square knots all around the ring.

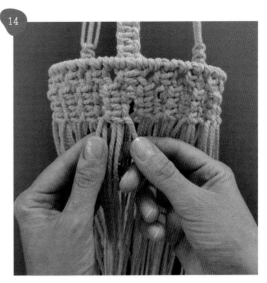

Starting between two of the previous square knots, make a sinnet of three consecutive square knots. Repeat this step all around the ring.

Starting between two of the sinnets of square knots, tie an alternating square knot to connect them. Repeat this step all around the ring.

Starting between two of the square knots from step 15, make another sinnet of three consecutive square knots. Repeat this step all around the ring.

Again, starting between the sinnets of step 16, tie alternating square knots to connect them. Repeat this step all around the ring.

Starting between two of the alternating square knots just made, one last time make another sinnet of three consecutive square knots. Repeat this step all around the ring.

Take the second 6-in. (15-cm) metal ring. Place it at the bottom edge of the last square knots.

Use the ring as a filler cord and attach it to the strands using double half hitch knots.

Take the 5¼-ft. (150-cm) cord. Bring all the strands together in the center and tie them together firmly with a gathering knot.

Cut the cords to the desired length to finish.

TIP

You can choose to use rings with a larger diameter. Simply add more cords in the spaces between the cords holding the metal ring.

CLASSIC OUTDOOR
Double Plant Hanger

Difficulty:

◆ ◆ ◇

Time required:
60 minutes

A hanger for twice the plant space and double the greenery! Ideal for both indoor and outdoor use.

TOOLS AND MATERIALS

- 1 pair of scissors

- 1 metal ring 2⅜ in. (6 cm) in diameter

- 6 pieces, ⅛ in. (3 mm) solid braided polypropylene rope (with core), 11 ft .(340 cm) long

- 2 pieces, ⅛ in. (3 mm) solid braided polypropylene rope (with core), 13 ft. (400 cm) long

- 2 pieces, ⅛ in. (3 mm) solid braided polypropylene rope (with core), 28 in. (70 cm) long

Take the metal ring. Attach the six 11-ft. (340-cm) cords, folded in half, to the ring using lark's head knots.

Take one of the 13-ft. (400-cm) cords and fold it so that one side is 5½ ft. (170) cm long and the other is 7½ ft. (230 cm) long. Place this cord on the far left and attach it to the ring with a lark's head knot, making sure the longest strand is on the outside left edge.

Take the second 13-ft. (400-cm) cord and repeat step 2, placing this cord on the far right, with a lark's head knot, making sure the longest strand is on the outside right edge.

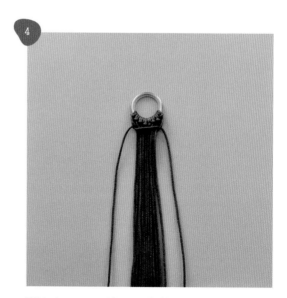

With the two outside strands (the ones longer than the others), make a first left-facing half square (spiral) knot around all the other cords to gather them all together. Tighten the knot firmly.

Make a total of twelve left-facing half square knots.

Separate the strands into groups of four.

With one group of four strands, drop down 4 in. (10 cm) and make a sinnet of ten left-facing half square knots to create a mini-spiral.

Repeat this step three more times.

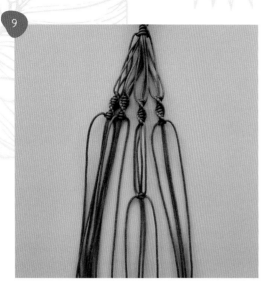

Drop down another 4 in. (10 cm). Tie a square knot.

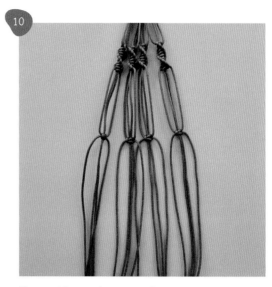

Repeat this step three more times.

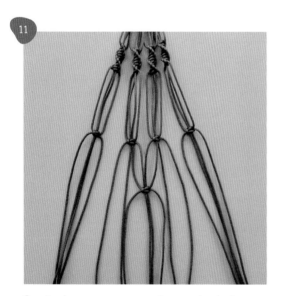

Starting between two square knots, take the last two and first two strands and, dropping down 2¾ in. (7 cm), tie an alternating square knot in the center.

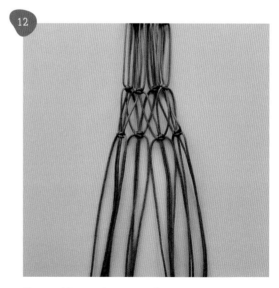

Repeat this step three more times.

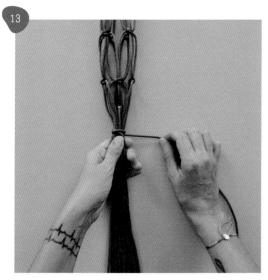

Take a 2¼-ft. (70-cm) cord. Drop down 2¾ in. (7 cm) below the last knot and tie all the cords together with a gathering knot.

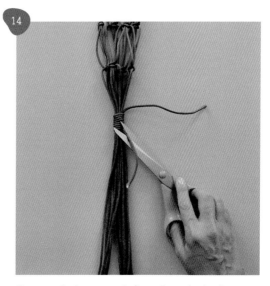

Cut strands that protrude from the gathering knot.

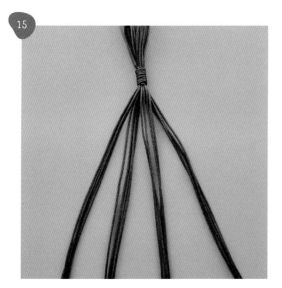

Again, separate your strands into groups of four. Be sure that each group has two short strands (in the center) and two long strands (on the outside).

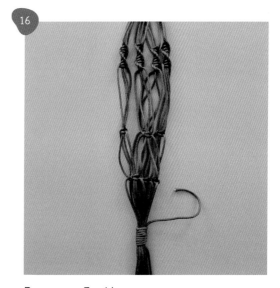

Repeat steps 7 to 14.

17

Cut the tassel to the desired length. Now it's finished!

TIP

You can add wooden beads in the middle of the spirals if you'd like.

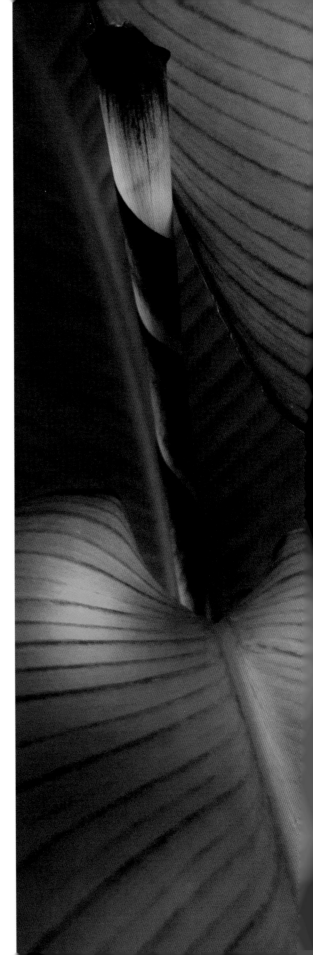

ABOUT THE AUTHOR

I n 2017, completely by chance, Virginie Pugliesi discovered the art of macramé for the first time, and she decided to learn more about this age-old practice.

Quickly won over by this craft, which she finds enriching and therapeutic, she threw herself into making her first projects, entirely self-taught. The hobby quickly became an addiction, which she then started sharing on Instagram, where she enjoys showing others her creations. Spurred on by the enthusiasm shown for her work and the encouragement from friends and family, she launched Place Boho, her online store for bohemian arts and crafts.

Passionate and constantly on the lookout for new designs, she has never stopped improving and expanding her art, which now includes interior design and items for special occasions or events. She shared her skills and expertise in her first tutorial book, *Macramé Bohème Folk* (Éditions Rustica, 2021), and with this new book embarked on another writing experience, with the aim of always inspiring people to discover macramé. You can find her creations on her website at www.placeboho.com or @place_boho on Instagram.

ACKNOWLEDGMENTS

I would first like to express my gratitude to my publisher Rustica, which has again entrusted me with this second project. Special thanks to Chloé, my editor; Julie, my artistic director; and Claire, my photographer, who have been with me since the first book and who have given me the opportunity to continue passing on my art.

A big thank-you also to my family: you are my first supporters. Your pride and your encouragement give me the audacity to always keep going, and if I'm where I am today, it's thanks to you.

I'd also like to express my gratitude to my friends, who have believed in Place Boho from the outset and have never stopped contributing to its development. Thank you for listening, advising, and supporting me all these years.

Finally, a big thank-you to you, my readers, my subscribers, and followers on my various social media platforms. It is thanks to you, and because so many of you enjoyed the first book, that the adventure continues. I am delighted to have inspired you to take the plunge and to have shared this passion with you. I hope that this second book will continue to inspire you and give you a lot of pleasure in the art of macramé.